Draw your portrait in the frame.

THIS BOOK BELONGS TO:

_____

_____

Tag and Share your Creations:

#ColorfulColoradoJournal

CHICAGO
REVIEW
PRESS

colorfulstates.com

ROCKY MOUNTAIN HIGH
COLORADO
—JOHN DENVER

Colorful Colorado

Welcome to colorful Colorado! 300 days of sunshine brighten the varied
landscape of canyons, rivers, mountains, plains, and sand dunes. Colorado is
home to 58 14,000+ foot mountain peaks, called "Fourteeners."

… THERE IS SOMETHING INFINITELY HEALING
IN THE REPEATED REFRAINS OF NATURE —
THE ASSURANCE THAT DAWN COMES AFTER NIGHT,
AND SPRING AFTER WINTER.

—RACHEL CARSON, *Silent Spring*

Steller's Jay + Blue Jays

An excellent mimic with a large repertoire, the jay can imitate birds, squirrels,
cats, dogs, chickens, and some mechanical objects. Steller's jays have black
heads and upper bodies, and live only in western North America.

STUDY NATURE,
LOVE NATURE,
STAY CLOSE TO NATURE.
IT WILL NEVER FAIL YOU.
—FRANK LLOYD WRIGHT

Greenback Cutthroat Trout

Colorado's state fish, and native species to the South Platte and Arkansas Rivers.
These fish are a lovely green color with dark spots and bright crimson stripes on
the sides of the throat. During spawning season, the entire belly may be red.

LOOK DEEP INTO NATURE
AND THEN YOU WILL UNDERSTAND
EVERYTHING BETTER.
—ALBERT EINSTEIN

Flatirons + Red Fox

Resourceful and cunning, the red fox is highly adaptable to wide varieties of habitat and diet. They can vary in color, but always have a white-tipped tail.

NORMALITY IS A PAVED ROAD;
IT'S COMFORTABLE TO WALK,
BUT NO FLOWERS GROW.

—VINCENT VAN GOGH

Rocky Mountain Columbine

Designated by school children to be the Colorado state flower back in 1899, this
white and blue columbine is loved by bees, hummingbirds, and butterflies alike.
To protect these popular flowers, it is illegal to uproot them on public lands.

TODAY IS YOUR DAY!
YOUR MOUNTAIN IS WAITING.
SO... GET ON YOUR WAY!

—DR. SEUSS

Elk in the Rocky Mountains

Elk are also called *wapiti*, a Native American (Shawnee) word that means
"white rump." They are large members of the deer family. Females are called
cows and males *bulls*. The bull's antlers can grow up to an inch a day.

IN EVERY WALK WITH NATURE
ONE RECEIVES FAR MORE
THAN HE SEEKS.

—JOHN MUIR

Abert's Squirrel

Also known as "squabbits," these adorable squirrels have large tufts of fur on
their ears and are grayish, reddish, or black with white undersides. They make
their home in ponderosa pines and get most their food from these trees.

OF ALL THE PATHS YOU TAKE IN LIFE,
MAKE SURE A FEW OF THEM ARE DIRT.

—JOHN MUIR

COLORADO STATE MAMMAL
Rocky Mountain Bighorn Sheep
1961

Bighorn Sheep

Both rams (males) and ewes (females) have curled horns. Males have larger horns, which they use as weapons for protection and dominance. Excellent vision and split hooves make them well-suited for life in the rough Rocky Mountain terrain.

EVERY SUNSET
BRINGS THE PROMISE
OF A NEW DAWN.
—RALPH WALDO EMERSON

Black Bear Sow and Cub

Black, brown, and even cinnamon in color, these intelligent creatures have a sense of
smell 7 times more powerful than a bloodhound. They can smell food up to 20 miles
away! In late fall, they eat 20,000 calories a day to prepare for winter hibernation.

NOT JUST BEAUTIFUL, THOUGH —
THE STARS ARE LIKE THE TREES IN THE FOREST,
ALIVE AND BREATHING. AND THEY'RE WATCHING ME.

—HARUKI MURAKAMI, *Kafka on the Shore*

Great Horned Owl Pair

Common to North America, these owls don't actually have horns at all,
but feathery tufts called *plumicorns*. Nighttime predators, these owls
have piercing yellow eyes and deep, soft hoots.

THOSE WHO DWELL AMONG THE BEAUTIES
AND MYSTERIES OF THE EARTH
ARE NEVER ALONE OR WEARY OF LIFE.
—RACHEL CARSON

Mule Deer

An icon of the American West, the mule deer's large ears are a key feature. It is
a graceful bounder, a motion called "stotting." Each bounce can be two feet high
and as long as 15 feet. This deer is an expert at navigating rough terrain.

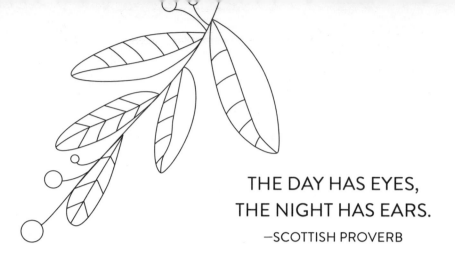

THE DAY HAS EYES,
THE NIGHT HAS EARS.

—SCOTTISH PROVERB

Mountain Cottontail Pair

The mountain cottontail inhabits the western US in grassy and wooded areas,
hopping, reproducing, and munching on grasses. Female mountain cottontails
are slightly larger than males, and they can have four to five litters a year.

SPRING IS NATURE'S WAY OF SAYING,
"LET'S PARTY!"
—ROBIN WILLIAMS

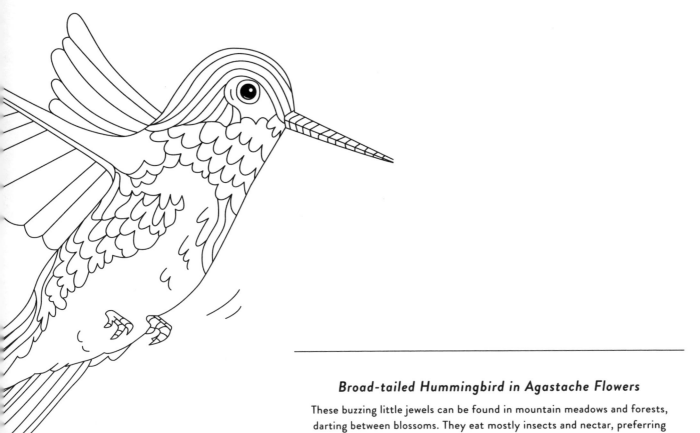

Broad-tailed Hummingbird in Agastache Flowers

These buzzing little jewels can be found in mountain meadows and forests,
darting between blossoms. They eat mostly insects and nectar, preferring
red tubular flowers such as the Agastache flowers.

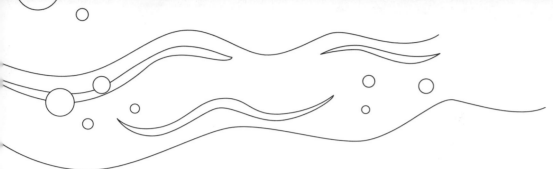

ADOPT THE PACE OF NATURE:
HER SECRET IS PATIENCE.

—RALPH WALDO EMERSON

Western Painted Turtle

In 2008, these bright turtles became Colorado's state reptile. They are common
dwellers among Colorado's ponds and lakes. With bright yellow and red markings
around the head and bottom shell, it's easy to see how they got their name.

HEAVEN IS UNDER OUR FEET
AS WELL AS OVER OUR HEADS.

—HENRY DAVID THOREAU, *Walden*

Moose

Moose are the largest member of the deer family. They are
a velvety chocolate brown. Their long legs help them swim,
traverse snowy meadows, and run at speeds of up to 35 mph.

I WONDER IF THE SNOW
LOVES THE TREES AND FIELDS,
THAT IT KISSES THEM SO GENTLY?
AND THEN IT COVERS THEM UP SNUG,
YOU KNOW, WITH A WHITE QUILT;
AND PERHAPS IT SAYS "GO TO SLEEP, DARLINGS,
TILL THE SUMMER COMES AGAIN."

—LEWIS CARROLL, *Through the Looking-Glass*

Canada Lynx

The lynx's long legs and distinctive large feet provide great mobility in
Colorado's snowy forests. These solitary creatures are protected under
the Endangered Species Act as a threatened species.

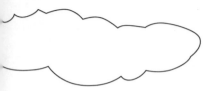

NATURE IS NOT
A PLACE TO VISIT.
IT IS HOME.
—GARY SNYDER

Coyotes

The coyote appears as a beloved trickster in many Native American tales.
They have cleverly adapted to change in the American landscape.
Thriving in urban and remote areas alike, they will eat almost anything.

ONE TOUCH OF NATURE
MAKES THE WHOLE WORLD KIN.

—WILLIAM SHAKESPEARE

Mountain Chickadees

Tiny and agile, these little birds dart through high branches of the mountains of
the West. Like all chickadees, they have black and white heads with gray wings.

COME FORTH INTO THE LIGHT OF THINGS,
LET NATURE BE YOUR TEACHER.

—WILLIAM WORDSWORTH

_____

Mountain Lion

A skilled solitary hunter, the mountain lion can reach speeds of up to 50 mph.
Their powerful hind legs enable them to jump as far as 45 feet.

WHEN WE TRY TO
PICK OUT ANYTHING BY ITSELF,
WE FIND IT HITCHED TO
EVERYTHING ELSE IN THE UNIVERSE.

—JOHN MUIR

Bumblebees in Bee Balm flowers

A bumblebee's wings beat 230 times or more per second. Because the bumblebee
is a threatened species, many people are planting bumblebee gardens and reducing
pesticides to try to save the habitat and food sources of this essential pollinator.

TO SIT IN THE SHADE ON A FINE DAY,
AND LOOK UPON VERDURE,
IS THE MOST PERFECT REFRESHMENT.

—JANE AUSTEN, *Mansfield Park*

Pika in the Maroon Bells

Pikas live at elevations above 11,000 ft. Their brown, pepper-colored fur lets
them blend into rocky terrain, where they create connected dens. They are
susceptible to global warming, moving higher in search of cool temperatures.

NATURE IS PLEASED WITH SIMPLICITY.
AND NATURE IS NO DUMMY.

—ISAAC NEWTON

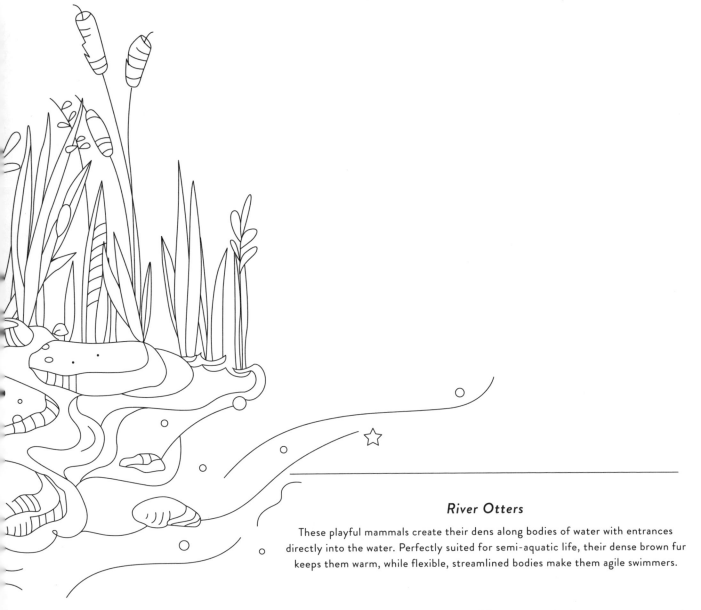

River Otters

These playful mammals create their dens along bodies of water with entrances directly into the water. Perfectly suited for semi-aquatic life, their dense brown fur keeps them warm, while flexible, streamlined bodies make them agile swimmers.

THE BEAUTY OF THE NATURAL WORLD LIES IN THE DETAILS.

—NATALIE ANGIER

Nighttime Raccoons

These creatures are often seen as devious and sneaky due to their nocturnal activity and signature black mask. The mask, however, may help reduce glare and aid the animal's nighttime vision.

THE POETRY OF THE EARTH
IS NEVER DEAD.

—JOHN KEATS

Lark Bunting Pair on Yucca Glauca

The Colorado state bird, the Lark bunting, is a common sparrow of the plains.
During mating season, the male is a distinctive black with white wing accents.
As winter approaches, his plumage becomes a striped gray/brown like the female.

NATURE GIVES TO EVERY TIME AND SEASON
SOME BEAUTIES OF ITS OWN.
—CHARLES DICKENS

Bison Family in the Northern Plains

The largest mammal in North America, the bison was almost hunted to extinction.
Recent efforts restored them to the plains of Colorado. Bison calves are born a
reddish-orange color that turns chocolate brown as they age.

NATURE ALWAYS WEARS
THE COLORS OF THE SPIRIT.
—RALPH WALDO EMERSON

Monarch Butterflies Resting on Cosmos

The monarch's distinctive orange, black, and white wings are beautiful, and warn predators that it is foul-tasting and poisonous. Notably, they make a 3,000 mile migration in the fall from east of the Rockies to Southern California and Mexico.

NATURE IS NEW EVERY MORNING.

—PROVERB

Mountain Goats at Overlook

These high altitude mammals are covered in a white, woolly coat. In the summer,
they live above treeline, often at elevations higher than 13,000 ft.
Males are called *billies*, females *nannies*, and their young *kids*.

I HAVE NEVER SEEN A WILDFLOWER
IN ALL ITS BEAUTY BE ASHAMED
OF WHERE IT GROWS.

—MICHAEL XAVIER

Indian Paintbrush and Alpine Avens Overlooking Mt. Sneffels

Castilleja, commonly known as Indian paintbrush, is a brilliant red/orange color,
although it can sometimes be rose, yellow, or white. The yellow alpine avens are
a common alpine flower. They are the favorite food of the Pika.

HAPPINESS FLUTTERS IN THE AIR
WHILST WE REST AMONG
THE BREATHS OF NATURE.

—KELLY SHEAFFER

Pronghorn Antelope

Pronghorns are some of the fastest animals in North America,
reaching speeds of up to 53 mph. They are a reddish brown color,
with white bellies and white bands across their necks.

ALL MY LIFE THROUGH,
THE NEW SIGHTS OF NATURE
MADE ME REJOICE LIKE A CHILD.

—MARIE CURIE

Yellow-bellied Marmots and View of Capitol Peak

A large member of the squirrel family, the yellow-bellied marmot can be up
to 2 feet long and weighs around 11 lbs. Their size and dense brown fur make
them well-suited to the cold, high-elevation areas where they live and burrow.

...EARTH, TEACH ME FREEDOM
AS THE EAGLE THAT SOARS IN THE SKY...
—UTE PRAYER

_____

Golden Eagle in Flight

This fast and nimble raptor is the ultimate predator of the skies. Magnificent in
flight, it is a rich brown color with a gold sheen at the back of the head and neck.
Many Native American tribes revere the golden eagle for its courage and strength.

AMANDA LENZ is a professional illustrator working and living in Boulder, Colorado. She paired her background in art and design with her love of the outdoors to develop the *Colorful Colorado Coloring Journal*, featuring rich, nature-inspired illustrations meant to be unique artworks.

Printed in the United States of America   0 9 8 7 6 5 4

Published by Chicago Review Press Incorporated
814 North Franklin Street
Chicago, Illinois 60610
ISBN 978-1-68275-159-6